This book belongs to ______________________

____

Traveling Sally Publications
www.travelingsally.com

National Library of Canada Cataloguing in Publication Data

Lambert, Sharon, 1979-
Sally the traveling hamster / written and illustrated by Sharon Lambert.

ISBN 0-9733099-0-3 (pbk.)

1. Hamsters--Juvenile fiction. I. Title.
PS8573.A3886S24 2003 jC813'.6 C2003-911004-4

Dedications

- In loving memory of my mom, who gave me the tools to succeed... faith, love, hope, and family.
- To my husband and family, for all their support and continual love.

Special thanks to photographer Nicholas Seiflow (Vancouver, BC)

Printed in Canada

Written and Illustrated by
Sharon Lambert

Traveling Sally Publications
www.travelingsally.com

I have a hamster named Sally

and she is the smartest Hamster of all.

Sally can do amazing things

even though she is small.

I taught her how to count to ten.
She asked me to teach her more.

Soon we were singing our ABC's
and Sally was spelling words galore.

I brought Sally to school in my backpack

so she could learn multiplication.

We learned about science, the stars
and the moon,

but her favorite was the puppet station.

Next we went to the Library.
It was full of books and maps.

I showed her all the countries and she said,
"I'll visit them all when I get a chance."

When we got home Sally climbed
into her hamster ball.

"I'm off to explore the World" She said,
"I want to see it all."

So Sally travels around the World,
learning all that she can.

Today I got a postcard from her.
Would you believe she's in Japan?

Everywhere that Sally goes
she learns something new.

I want to keep on learning and see
what amazing things I can do.

The

End !!

ᵕ

Sally the traveling Hamster

by Sharon Lambert

Postcard from Sally in

Hello from Japan,

I'm learning how to write Japanese.

山 This means mountain.

I think these three lines look like three tall mountains.

What do you think?